The Serpent's Lie

Miguel A. Valembrun Jr.

Copyright © 2018 Miguel A. Valembrun Jr.

All rights reserved.

ISBN: 978-1-950773-00-8

DEDICATION

To my God and King who gives me purpose,

my lovely wife who supports me in every sensible endeavor including this dream of mine to become an author,

my loving mother who encourages me and continues to teach me that selfless acts are more valuable than titles and accolades,

my father who planted a few philosophical and poetic seeds in the garden of my mind,

my grandmother who spent countless hours praying over the family,

and my four wonderful sisters who provoke thought and spark intellectual exchanges

They say behind every great man is a great woman. Whether or not, I ever become "great", I will remember always that among some noteworthy men (whom I've been blessed to call friends and family), there is a platoon of exceptional women who helped me grow into the man I've become.

CONTENTS

	INTRODUCTION	Pg 5
1	Chapter one	Pg 10
2	Chapter two	Pg 18
3	Chapter three	Pg 25
4	Chapter four	Pg 30
5	Chapter five	Pg 38
6	Chapter six	Pg 44
7	Chapter seven	Pg 52
8	Chapter eight	Pg 60
9	Chapter nine	Pg 69
10	Chapter ten	Pg 74
11	Chapter eleven	Pg 77
12	Chapter twelve	Pg 82
13	Chapter thirteen	Pg 86
14	Chapter fourteen	Pg 90
15	Chapter fifteen	Pg 97

INTRODUCTION

What if this world isn't what we have been told it is; the result of one favorable chance against an astronomical sea of unfavorable odds? What if its true origin is more extraordinary and miraculous than we had been led to believe? How would we adapt to our new reality once we discovered it?

The truth is we are not an accident—not a random event triggered by chaos and probability. Instead, we were created purposefully by a higher intelligence whom we call God.

Somehow, we forgot our origins. We have been searching the stars for answers which have been in front of us since time began. I know this because not too long ago, I was doing the same. Now, however, I know beyond a shadow of doubt that God created us. He is real and this book is the first of a series that I hope will help you understand Biblical truth like never before. Now, you are probably wondering why you should even trust me on this journey; after all, you may not know me...so here's a little bit about me:

I was brought up in a Christian home and taught that the Bible is the authentic and inspired word of God. Period! My family and I attended church weekly because mom and dad said so. In silent protest to my required attendance, my body was often present in church almost every Sunday, while my mind was often absent. Like many, I had questions and doubts and often felt like my time and mental faculties were being wasted on trying to imagine an invisible deity. Ironically, when "religion" seemed too overbearing, I often escaped into the wonderful realm of myths and legends from all around the world many of which bear similarities to the accounts of the Bible. Once upon a time, many of them were active religions too.

In the back of my mind, I always believed in **a** god. It made sense to me that just as buildings and cars have makers, this world was created. But as I became more familiar with other religions and searched for "alternative truths", I became more conflicted. What made the God of the Bible more authentic than other gods? Were gods even real or were they all figments imagined by superstitious and imperialistic minds?

I furthered my independent studies, seeking truth from the world of science. Science was factual, consistent, and trustworthy after all, at least that's what I was taught. Cars, computers, cell phones, and the entire lifestyle of developed societies was made possible by the application of science. So, if it worked, it had to be truth! Furthermore, its noble quest was to spread enlightenment to the world and free minds that had been enslaved by superstition. One of its missions was also mine — to ultimately discover the cause and purpose of our existence. Soon, however, it became clear that as noble as pure science might be, the most *influential* scientists around tend to be anti-God, anti-Christ, and anti-Christian.

For them, our origin is Godless. Although the probability of God's existence is infinitely greater than the probability of a random cell appearing out of nowhere billions of years ago, the Big Bang *theories* and the *theory* of Evolution prevail over the acknowledgement of a Divine Creator. For the record, random cells cannot appear out of nowhere, fully assembled and somehow pre-programmed to survive and thrive. That would be impossible! Fortunately for truth seekers, precarious rules do not govern our reality. Rather, the steadfast rules set by God determine possibilities and constraints here on earth. If you think about it, no human being in history has ever witnessed anything appear out of nowhere except bad drivers, magic show attendees, and witnesses of both demonic, and divine activity.

The moment that I resolved to give God the benefit of the doubt, I revisited the Bible. I'll admit the accounts still seemed somewhat mythical. One immensely powerful entity allegedly creates the Heavens and the earth, then creates all living beings in pairs along with the most famous human couple Adam and Eve. He places them in a garden and sets some ground rules which they end up disobeying. They are consequently punished, and mortality and sin enter the world. Why would anyone believe this and turn a "logically" inclined ear, toward this far-fetched account? Perhaps because the account is surprisingly more accurate than we often realize!

This book is not for everyone. It presents historical accounts that have been withheld from many and fresh perspectives that can help to demystify the Bible. In August of 2016, a passion greater than anything I had ever felt compelled me to start writing "The Serpent's Lie". Believers in the LORD refer to such urges as 'a calling on one's life'. My God created me with a purpose that I was just beginning to understand.

At first, it was supposed to be a spiritually therapeutic book of Biblical promises. Over time, however, it became something else. It challenged my faith and greatly increased it. It also challenged my critical thought, evoking questions that God always answered in various ways until I realized that the contents of the Bible could **not** have been imagined by human beings. In fact, many passages of scripture contain concepts that are far too advanced for our ancient ancestors to have even contemplated!

If you've made it this far, then this book was written for a curious mind like yours. I pray that you enjoy my very first book and find life-changing truth in "The Serpent's Lie".

CHAPTER 1

The Transient Life

When man was first created, he did not know death. He lived in perfect peace in a perfect world. This was long before corruption, pollution, carcinogens, climate change, and so on. This was a time before the history which we have been taught; a time before we were told how to think.

Nowadays, every square inch of our world has been touched by corruption. Foods grown from the richest soil have long lost their primordial ability to perpetually prolong our lifespans! Regrettably, despite the pollution and toxicity surrounding us, we tend to believe that anyone who reaches or exceeds the human life expectancy has lived to a ripe old age, but our perception of "old" is relative.

Have you ever stopped and wondered why modern people can't live two or three times longer? Have you ever wondered why we all must die? Let us take time to consider the following:

Many archeological discoveries, thus far, reveal our ancient ancestors were more durable than we are today. According to the Bible, however, not only were they strong, but many also thrived for several centuries at a time! By comparison, our modern life expectancy is rather unimpressive.

Science seeks (among many things) to understand the phenomenon which we call "Death", yet we do not currently have an answer to the riddle of death, nor a solution to stop it. Research has led us to many *theories*, but they all seem to point to an internal cause. For example, the length of our telomeres has been theorized to correlate with the expected length of our lives. For more information, please feel free to read the following article:

Genetic Science Learning Center. (2016, March 1) Are Telomeres the Key to Aging and Cancer. Retrieved October 11, 2018, from https://learn.genetics.utah.edu/content/basics/telomeres/

Telomeres are regions at the ends of chromosomes that prevent them from deteriorating or fusing with other chromosomes. They can be compared to the plastic ends of a shoelace that prevent its tips from fraying. In a similar manner, telomeres preserve genetic information by preventing the tips of chromosomes from disintegrating or fusing together. Unfortunately, as we age, telomeres get shorter and errors begin to occur with increasing frequency.

The free radical theory is another theory that attempts to explain the mechanisms behind death. It suggests that microscopic particles called free radicals, ricochet off internal structures within our cells resulting in cellular damage. It further suggests that we may be able to slow the rate of damage by ingesting antioxidant-rich foods and beverages. This would result in an increased life expectancy. For more information on the free radical theory, please feel free to read the following article:

Villines, Z. (2017, July 29). "How do free radicals affect the body?." Medical News Today. Retrieved from https://www.medicalnewstoday.com/articles/318652.php

While these current theories might help us better understand the aging process and combat it, understanding them only helps us delay the inevitable. We have yet to reconcile ourselves with the origin, purpose, and modus operandi of death as the theories mentioned earlier do not account for them. If anti-aging theories cannot provide the answers we seek, then something else can—the Bible.

According to the Bible, Death was "born" in a place called Eden. Its purpose was to prevent mankind from being trapped in an immortal and defiled condition. Its modus operandi was to alter the human genome to include a "mortal trait". In this way, our once genetically perfect ancestors would become imperfect molds that would reproduce imperfect offspring. This was half of the formula. The second half guaranteed a finite lifespan via a curse which was placed upon the very earth we live on. From the moment death was brought into our existence, the earth would no longer yield the perfect sustenance we needed in order to live forever. On a microscopic level, cells, tissues, muscles, and other components within the body would gradually decline irreversibly.

If you've ever been cut or injured so badly that it left a permanent mark, then you might have already been aware of the following fact:

The body <u>does not</u> completely heal injury.

The extent of our recovery from injuries depends on how well they are treated, but expectations of "full recoveries" are unrealistic. We have heard the term before, but no such events exist; if they did, then we would be immortal. In other words, all wear, tear, and damage to our bodies would be restored to mint condition. We would be like cars that remained brand new no matter how much they were driven! Obviously, we know this is not the case. Therefore, despite the quality of our genes and/or diets, we are all finite.

Death has proven itself to be unerringly consistent, so much so, in fact, that not one single creature has **ever** escaped its reach. Consider this for a moment. Not ONE. Instead, we all have learned to accept it as an inevitable part of life.

Now what if I told you immortality is real, and it once existed here on earth? Would you believe me? I would not fault you if you didn't because the concept of immortality defies what we have perceived throughout our lives. Nevertheless, let us entertain this idea and suppose it to be real. If immortality exists somewhere outside of this mortal realm, our next question should be "why not here?" The answer is—because nothing can exist where it is not allowed to. Immortality here on earth is no different!

THE SERPENT'S LIE

Imagine we lived in a perfect world with perfect nutrition. In such a world, life could be sustained **eternally**. You see, food replenishes us with the energy we expend, and nutrients from food go toward restoration from the daily wear and tear of our physical activities.

When one sleeps, the body self-repairs using the energy harnessed from the food it consumed. Therefore, a richer diet usually corresponds with greater health; but a body sustained by what we consider to be poor nutrition, tends to lack the nutrients needed to effectively self-repair. We have already established that full recoveries do not exist. Even so, let's imagine not just *good* nutrition, but a **_perfect— complete_** type that could restore us **fully**! With such nutrition, our bodies would be perpetually renewed with each meal!

Alas, not a single thing can exist in an environment that does not permit it to. Perfect nutrition (or perfect anything for that matter) cannot exist in a defiled environment. Thus, corruption like most other transmittable things, flows from areas of higher concentration to areas of lower concentration. In this manner, conditions such as disease cannot thrive in a perfect world, just as perfection could not *thrive* in a diseased world.

Allow me to illustrate this point:

If we put a single microorganism (such as a cell) in a petri dish with lethal chemicals, it would absorb those chemicals then die. It would **not** be permitted to exist and persist in such an environment. However, if we put the same cell in a hospitable environment it would thrive. Likewise, if we scaled the petri dish to the size of our world and we became the microorganisms by comparison, we would see much more clearly how our external environment influences our longevity and well-being. We have little say in the matter! It is a fundamental law of existence that nurturing environments promote life whereas toxic ones lead to decline and then death.

With that said, we are all malnourished. Perhaps you had never dared to consider this fact prior to now; for the common and present-day standard of malnourishment is an anorexic, bloated-bellied individual from photos reminiscent of third world life. We have been taught that this is the appearance of poorly nourished people when in fact, we are simply comparing their more deficient diets to our own. Even so, every one of us is malnourished because the ground cannot fully sustain life as it was once able to.

So where did death specifically come from? The answer to this question is surprisingly simple; like everything else, it was created by God!

CHAPTER 2

A Trip to the Primordial Past

The average life expectancy of the global population is approximately 72 years from birth, according to a 2016 study conducted by the World Health Organization (WHO). This "longevity" is due largely to modern nutritional and health sciences which have helped us combat the negative impacts of pollution as well as the overall declining quality of food.

According to "Dirt Poor: Have Fruits and Vegetables Become Less Nutritious?" published by Scientific American, "fruits and vegetables grown decades ago were much richer in vitamins and minerals than the varieties most of us get today."

www.scientificamerican.com/article/soil-depletion-and-nutrition-loss/

Some other sources have confirmed the decline of food quality. Two such sources are as follows:

https://www.momsacrossamerica.com/stunning_corn_comparison_gmo_versus_non_gmo

https://www.ncbi.nlm.nih.gov/pubmed/15637215

An honest review of the past would reveal that the world was cleaner (overall) and healthier. Some exceptional events could make us think otherwise—events such as the Plague of Justinian and the Black Death (both of which were Bubonic Plagues caused by **Yersinia pestis, a bacterium carried in Oriental rats and their fleas**). Such isolated events occurred as a result of inadequate knowledge of communal hygiene along with an unawareness of microorganisms and proper waste disposal. Aside from those, however, the world was indeed cleaner. If pollution has only *increased* (plastic bottles, oil spills, carbon emissions, etc.), along with diseases, birth defects, cancers, etc., then there must have been less pollution along with its side effects in the past.

Imagine you and I traveling back in time through the ages. We witness a reversal of deforestation and watch as cars and highways disappear from existence. Shortly afterwards, you start to feel some weird biorhythmic changes which you can't quite put your fingers on—but I'll help you. Let's start with your breath, focus on the inflow and outflow. Do you feel it? Every inhalation excites you and fills you with ever increasing energy levels you've only dreamed of!

Asthma and respiratory problems have been left in the distant future where humans and animals breathe filthy smog. Diseases like cancer have also been left behind in the future of toxicity. A strange almost supernatural change has occurred within you. You now feel more resilient as allergies are now a thing of the bygone future. The earth has become cleaner and more naturally fertile. As a result, flowers have blossomed ubiquitously. As we hurtle backwards in time, the environment becomes increasingly pure and approaches perfection. Our time machine slows to a halt. We have reached the earliest accessible point in time ... Genesis ... our stop. After having travelled several millennia, we now find ourselves amid a vibrant and verdant world replete with life. We are in a place called Eden.

Eden, the most beautiful place we have ever seen, assaults our unaccustomed eyes. Before we can take it all in, however, something flickering from our peripheral snatches our attention. We adjust our view and behold a bright light swirls around a blob of clay whose silhouette seems strangely familiar to us. This clay figure appears to have bilateral symmetry. Moreover, it appears to be bipedal and anthropomorphic.

As the light dances around the sculpture, we begin to realize it is alive ... not the sculpture, but the light! It is a thinking being that is adding detail to the form at an alarming rate! Within seconds, what had previously been a round and unidentifiable part of the sculpture begins to resemble a human face complete with closed eyelids, a nose, mouth, cheeks, and ears. As we marvel at this artistry, a powerful breeze rustles through the garden and suddenly, a warmth of color perfuses the sculpture replacing what was previously a vapid visage with a warm colored one. It is alive!... I am no longer referring to the light, but to the sculpture! What you and I have just witnessed was the creation of man. Of course, this rendition (no matter how magical it sought to be) could not capture the long-forgotten marvel and majesty of this historical event.

When man was first created, he was immortal, and he knew paradise! His maker, a being who embodies light and perfection, had planted a garden wherein he placed the newly formed man. The light being gave him the responsibility to care for the garden and as he maintained it, the garden would express its appreciation of the man by supplying him with perfect sustenance. There was, however, one problem with his life at this point—he was alone! He was the first and sole member of his kind at the time. The light being did not enjoy seeing him alone, so it created a partner which the man called "woman" and together, they became the first generation of humankind. The new couple dwelt in the perfectly peaceful paradise of Eden.

One day, an evil entity slipped into the garden. This entity was a sworn enemy of the Light Being and influenced the first man and woman to disobey their creator. This evil one persuaded them to eat of a special tree which had been forbidden by their maker. This tree, "The Tree of Knowledge of Good and Evil" bore a species of fruit which were able to impart increased awareness to the eater. The fruit did not have any other purpose, such as boosting the immune system or providing energy. Rather, they supplied a level of knowledge which mankind had not been prepared to acquire. As a matter of fact, the maker had specifically warned him not to eat of it for in the day that he would taste of the fruit, he would certainly die. But as the account goes, the man and the woman wound up eating of it anyway. As a result, they were expelled from the garden and from then on, they were supposedly cursed to live a mortal life of hard labor and despair.

The story summarized above was the account of Adam and Eve and the event which became known as the "fall of mankind". The one referred to as "the Maker" and "Light Being" is better known as "the LORD God", El Elyon "the Most High", Yahweh, the "LORD of Hosts", and a plethora of other names. The Tree of the Knowledge of Good and Evil was a tree that was staged by the

LORD in the middle of the garden and the only one that man (both Adam and Eve) could not eat from. The "evil" that entered the garden has been called many names, especially in the various translations of the Bible, but perhaps the most well-known of all because of the influence of Latin translations, would be "Lucifer", the one we now call Satan.

Lucifer whose name was translated into Latin from the Hebrew, *Helel Ben Sachar*, was once regarded as the bearer of light (from the Latin: lux, luc- meaning 'light' + -ferre meaning ' to bear / carry'), but lost that title after rebelling against the LORD some time before the era of man. Therefore, he is no longer worthy to be called by former names since he no longer bears true light. He is, however, still able to masquerade as an angel of light (refer to 2 Corinthians 11:14). More appropriately, after his rebellion, Lucifer became the "Wicked One", "the ancient serpent called the Devil", "the Accuser", "Ha-Satan", or simply "Satan" (meaning "the Adversary") for he is the chief enemy of God and humankind.

Perhaps it's strange that a book like this should begin with death, the promise, and the transgression that brought it into being. After all, God began everything by bringing life. Still, death appears in Genesis, the very book that recounts the creation of the heavens, the earth, and all living things.

We know a promise is a declaration that something will happen. Thus, when God declared that death would surely befall mankind if Adam and Eve ate of the fruit, He spoke the very first promise known to man. Death is the first example that God ALWAYS keeps His word (whether it is good or seemimgly bad); for every living thing on earth lives for a time and then dies. It's simple! It has been declared, written, —**PROMISED**. We are at the mercy of time, nature, and various natural processes while we exist in flesh. Then we die.

CHAPTER 3

Common Objections

What sort of "loving" God would curse a creature that He had designed? This is a question that many people ask after reading the story of Adam and Eve.

The fall of the first couple and mankind (through them) is a bitter pill to swallow. It is so bitter, in fact, that many people are not willing to accept it. Denial has swept the world because no one wants to hear that they have fallen short of anything. More specifically, nobody wants to hear that they have sinned and fallen short of the glory of God, (myself included). Therefore, many of us find it hard to admit this fact to ourselves. Truth, however, is no less true because it hurts the one(s) who hear it. Additionally, many people deny the account of Man's fall as told in Genesis because they cannot comprehend how one couple's sin has affected the entirety of human beings, plant, and animal species throughout the ages. To make matters worse, why was that darned tree even there?!

Why had God in his alleged infinite wisdom placed one single forbidden tree in the garden of Eden? Wasn't a fall from glory an obvious inevitability? After all, Adam and Eve had lived in a vast, yet limited space (the face of the earth) and they had unlimited life expectancy at the time. Therefore, they had unlimited opportunities to taste of the forbidden fruit. So logically, what could have kept humans forever uninterested in the tree?

We can ask a plenitude of questions, some of which, quite frankly, are trivial. We can place so much focus, *not* on the details that make the story credible, but on the ones that make it unbelievable to us. This tendency coupled with a preexisting aversion to God, may result in asking questions with the goal of disproving the annals of the Bible instead of seeking to gain clarity. As a result, we often end up losing sight of broader ideas. In this case, the broader idea is the plain and simple fact that Adam and Eve disobeyed the LORD!

When God created man and placed him in the garden of Eden, He tasked him with dressing and keeping it. In other words, Adam was to maintain it. Although God initially gave humans dominion and freedom to enjoy everything on earth (except for one thing), everything was ultimately the LORD's. The sharing of power was analogous to the owner of a company hiring a President and Vice President to oversee its operation. Before the owner went on vacation, he told the presidents that they had unlimited access to all company resources...except one. It should not matter if the one forbidden resource had been placed in the middle of their office nor hidden away. The presidents were given a command from someone whose authority superseded theirs.

Therefore, if the president or vice president disobeyed the command of the owner, most people would understand any consequences that followed up to and including termination. When it comes to the garden, however, we don't want to hear Adam disobeyed, do we? Instead, we want to know why God placed the tree there, how the fruit looked, whether it was an apple, a pomegranate, or a grape. Can you believe that scholars are still trying to figure out what species of fruit were on the forbidden tree?

Dear reader, the Bible (which is often regarded as one very large book) contains **sixty-six** books that are replete with historical details! In other words, it is quite hefty enough! However, some among us are convinced that it should have even more details! Again, we can ask many questions such as "How tall was the tree?", "Was it of a tropical variety (like a palm tree)?", or "What species of fruit did it bear?" but *we will **never** have **all** the information.* Furthermore, there are an infinite number of questions we can ask.

If the Bible contained all the information we often think it needs, it would be egregiously lengthy and unreadable! Besides, let's be real for a second; no account is ever <u>fully</u> detailed because some bits of info are unnecessary. Consider the following scenario for a moment:

A motor vehicle accident occurs and one of the drivers recounts the event. How likely will the driver be to explain the wind speed or the song on his radio leading up to the moment of impact? Not likely at all! The fact of the matter is that two motor vehicles crashed into each other! Likewise, the species of fruit that Adam and Eve ate is unnecessary along with the detailed reasoning behind the tree's existence inside of the garden. These tidbits of info do not concern us. The fact of the matter is that the serpent lied, and Adam and Eve disobeyed their Creator!

If there's one thing to know about the promises of God, it is that **they are dependable.** He always ensures the outcome of that which He speaks. For example, when He said to man, "...for in the day that you eat thereof you shall surely die", death became a certainty for Adam, Eve, and all living things on Earth from the day in which man disobeyed.

The account of the human fall is not an easy one to read. To be quite honest, the Bible *is not for* our entertainment *(per se)*. It exists to teach us more about our Heavenly Father, how sin interferes in our relationship with Him, and that He is our Savior. The Bible **becomes** a priceless resource when we read it with humility, submit to our God, and learn to live by faith. The expected result is a restored relationship with our maker and spiritual growth.

CHAPTER 4

Addressing Objections

In order to avoid some common pitfalls, especially at the start of their "walk" with the LORD, believers will often have to get past several initial objections such as the following:

- "Adam and Eve didn't even die **<u>on</u>** that day like God said they would!"

- "Why did God punish everyone?"

- "The Bible blames women for the fall and uses this as a basis to subject women to men."

- "Why is God referred to with masculine pronouns?"

Dear reader, if you will kindly stick with me, I endeavor to make the book of Genesis and the promises it contains clearer to a modern audience than it has ever been made before. I also aim to dispel many common misconceptions that might prevent our acceptance of biblical truth.

Let us now consider the objections in the order in which they were listed.

#1. "They didn't even die on that day."

When reading the account of mankind's fall from glory, many believe the Bible is inaccurate from the start because man did not die ***on*** that day as God said he would. First, please understand that the Bible has been translated from other languages. One can argue that a mistranslation may have occurred, but before we entertain the idea of a mistranslation, let us consider the New King James version and its wording. This version, widely considered to be one of the most accurate translations to date, says **"in** the day" as opposed to **"on** the day". There is a gigantic connotative difference between the two. In case you don't see it yet, the difference will be clarified through the following example:

- "in those days people sacrificed cattle"

- "on those days people sacrificed cattle"

Do you see the difference? One of those examples connotes an era or timespan **in which** cattle was sacrificed. The other connotes specific days of the week **on which** cattle were sacrificed. So perhaps it is not a matter of mistranslation but a simple misunderstanding of the connotation. This is but the first rebuttal.

Second, anyone who mistakenly considers God's first promise as a "broken one" should understand that death is a process. Metaphorically speaking, Death is a blackout that occurs city block by city block. If God had said to Adam "for in the day that you eat thereof you will surely grow", every reader would anticipate a *process* of growth and not a sudden transformation from normal human stature to multi-story gigantism. Just like growth, death is a *process*; therefore, our idea of it needs adjustment. For some reason, when we think of death, we imagine an instant stoppage of life. Let's imagine instead black weed vines spreading across a host as a representation of death.

Life is not an instant spark of consciousness. Rather, it is a span of existence. Its "rival" (Death) therefore, does not instantly snuff out its flame but instead subtracts from it until the flame of life ceases to exist. Every illness, every injury, every bad nutrient, and all compounded wear upon the body leads each of us closer to our inevitable demise.

It has been said that from the moment we are born, we are already dying. This saying more accurately depicts death as anything but instantaneous, though even more accurately (in my opinion), life triumphs over death time and again in the prime years of our lives. We get stronger from infancy into young adulthood, defying death's grip, but in the second half of our lives, death gains the advantage. We reach a zenith after which, we begin to decline. Either way, it is a process. Let's revisit the passage with some new understanding and paraphrase it.

God warned Adam not to eat of the fruit:

"For from the moment that he would eat thereof ... in that era, mortality would make itself known to Adam. Life would start to depart from him. As it left him, death would take its hold."

Now do we see how God's first promise was fulfilled? It would have been the end of human history if Adam and Eve had instantly been stricken by sudden death! Of what benefit then, would a Bible ever have been if Adam and Eve did not live long enough to multiply? What good would it have served in a world without souls descended from them? This is but the second rebuttal.

Finally, my third counterargument to the notion that Adam and Eve's death did not occur immediately enough is that the word death doesn't always refer to a physical event. If any death had been instant, it was Adam's spiritual death.

Many people "die" before their bodies do. We have heard the expression "dead man walking", we have seen people who are hopeless, or even cold and loveless. People like that have suffered a spiritual death of a figurative sort. So, when Adam ate from the fruit, God's promise manifested itself as the immediate but figurative death of his spirit which became separated or estranged from the Creator. If God was the Supreme source of life for man, then sin severed the spiritual 'filament' that had constantly fed immortal life into mankind. It was **in** that day that a gradual shutdown began to occur.

#2) Why did God punish everyone?

It is to the glory and honor of any builder to see a work of his hands function as designed. Man, as a work of God, was no different. Adam and Eve had become depraved by knowledge that should, according to Satan, have made them more divine, like the Most High. However, God still wanted everything to continue as it was. He intended to fix the mess in due time, but first, humankind had to be taught some valuable lessons. One of these lessons, is how to put our trust in the Lord despite our limited understanding and the influences of others. Some other lessons are:

THE SERPENT'S LIE

- The value of life

- The value of relationships among family and friends

- What it means to experience suffering

- Having hope during times of suffering or gloom

- Having faith in ideals that are greater than ourselves

- Learning patience (which only happens when our faith and hope have been tested)

Surely, we live in an imperfect world, but God knows exactly why He made the tough calls that He did and whether we like to hear it or not, He *was* more than fair to us when He made them.

We all experience the punishment of death because, as odd as it is to contemplate, we were ALL involved in the sin. We all were in Adam during the time of his fall. We were among the billions of cells that comprised his form. When God pronounced Adam and Eve's punishment, the sentence of mortality was spoken to every cell that they consisted of, including the reproductive ones! Thus, we were all brought into mortal being via the seeds of Adam. The mortal trait, which is also the sentence of death, was passed along on a cellular level! Perfection, you see, could no longer thrive in something that had been corrupted.

Through Adam and Eve all human life would be brought forth, and so all lives had been in them when corruption entered this world. In addition, the very first time that we did something against the conscience, whether it was a white lie, small theft, impure thought, etc. we proved that we were no different from our first ancestors. We proved that we were also fallible and worthy of the same penalty as they were … and so death manifests itself to all flesh.

#3) The Bible blames women for the Fall and uses it as a basis to subject women to men.

Anyone who speaks such a sentence is **<u>highly</u>** misinformed. To better understand Eve's role in the Fall, we must understand the second chapter of Genesis. Eve whom the LORD had taken from Adam and formed into a distinct consciousness is not said to have been warned by God. Though the human couple "vibed" on one spiritual frequency, Eve was her own person. God had commanded Adam not to eat of the tree. In the third chapter, after Eve had been created, an Adversary in the form of a serpent, stepped in to deceive her. He chose her because he knew she was more likely to believe his lies. He knew this, not because she was more gullible than Adam, but because she had not directly received the LORD's command. As expected, she ate the forbidden fruit then shared with Adam, the one whom the LORD had directly spoken to.

It was Adam who had knowingly eaten from the fruit and in so doing, **he** had deliberately disobeyed. The Bible is clear, for anyone who wishes to blame the fall of mankind on a woman:

1 Timothy 2:14 (KJV)
14 And Adam was not deceived, but the woman being deceived was in the transgression.

In other words, Eve was tricked but Adam participated knowing very well what God had instructed. The Bible does not blame her. Unfortunately for Eve, however, she was still "in the transgression", meaning she was still involved.

CHAPTER 5

The Divine Gender Identity

One of the biggest challenges to accepting Biblical truth in our day and age is accepting God's gender identity. I once had a conversation with a female acquaintance about God's gender. "How could God be male if females give life?", she asked. I acknowledged the validity of her question and reasoned that God could perhaps be a Supreme "It" since everything, male and female came from Him. This was before I better understood the reason why the sexes exist. Years later, I finally realized that a fe_male_ is a particular pattern of male; a wo_man_ is a particular pattern of man, and s_he_ is a particular pattern of he — all because God originally made woman from man.

The Bible's reference to God using masculine pronouns is indeed controversial for some. This is due in large part to societal sensitivities linked to unequal treatment of women throughout history. However, before we confuse God with man, God states matter of factly that He is not a man:

THE SERPENT'S LIE

"God is not a man that He should lie..." Numbers 23:19

"For I am God, and not man…" Hosea 11:9

In those statements, He speaks broadly, clarifying the fact that He is not human...let alone a man. Nevertheless, He uses masculine pronouns. In order to get past the hurdles caused by our sensitivities toward gender, let us first consider a linguistic property that emerged with language itself and has endured to this very day.

Masculine and feminine pronouns are used commonly (even for non-personal nouns) in languages such as Spanish, French, and even English! In Spanish, for instance, a book is masculinized (un libro), a table is feminized (una mesa). Yet we know the masculinization and feminization of objects have nothing to do with elevating one gender over another. In English, nature is often feminized (Mother Nature) as are other things like boats and ships. This does not ruffle any feathers, for it is regarded purely as a linguistic property. When God is masculinized, however, things change, and feelings are hurt...but we need to get over it. A pronoun is ultimately nothing more than a word.

The LORD God is neither a man nor a woman. Rather, *"God is spirit, and His worshipers must worship in the Spirit and in truth."*, according to John 4:24. If we paraphrase that verse, while understanding that the Bible is the written and Holy-Spirit-inspired word of God, we realize that the LORD refers to Himself as a masculine spirit. As believers, we tend to just go with the things written in the Bible, but I do not want us to do that today. Instead, I would like for us to engage in thought and derive the answers from the scripture.

"Why does the Bible refer to God by using masculine pronouns?"

One can simply answer "Well, because it does" but this will not get us anywhere. We must analyze the question to obtain a proper answer.

Knowing that the Bible (God's written and inspired word) implies God is—not a man—but masculine, we should rephrase the original question as *"Why does the word of God refer to Him with masculine pronouns?"*. From there, we can rephrase it one last time as *"Why does God, Himself (since the Bible is recognized as His written word), imply He is masculine?"*

For the answer, let us understand two more things:

1. the reason why genders exist in the first place

2. their intended interplays.

We will understand those through the following Biblical fact:

Eve was extracted from Adam.

I know you may have questions, maybe even objections, but you will soon find that as strange as the Genesis account might seem, it agrees with **real** science—not theories but actual...factual science. You will discover that the Bible agrees with science up to the point where scientific theory, lies, and misinformation attempt to remove God from the equation of existence.

You see, we never evolved from primates, as the *theory* of evolution wrongly supposes! Rather, earth's increasing population gives us clues about our origins. If more people came from less people, then we can deduce that the population would decrease if we reversed time. Did you know the world population in the year 1750 was only 700 million people? That was only 270 years prior to 2019 where the world population was 7.7, almost 8 billion people! In other words, within less than 3 centuries of forward time travel, the population grew by more than 1000 percent! If we could reverse time, the population would decline 1000% by 1750, and if we could travel far enough into the past, I have no doubt that we would find the two people responsible for starting the cycle of human reproduction. For those who do not currently believe in the Bible, you can call those two people whatever you want...Robert and Ann, Simon and Julie etc....As for me, however, since the Bible calls them "Adam and Eve" I'll just go with its flow.

The Genesis account explains the nature of the human pair.

When we look at Genesis 5:2 we notice that although male and female were separate, God saw Adam and Eve as one entity. As a result, He initially called them Adam. Adam, the man himself, called his other half Eve. Whereas Adam saw the physical separation, God saw the oneness of origin, and the singularity of perfect compatibility.

Male and female He created them; and blessed them, and called **their name** *"Adam", in the day when they were created.* - Gen 5:2

Did you see that?!

God called the first **couple** the name of the man because Eve had been extracted from Adam! Since then humankind is still considered "Adam" in Hebrew; because his name means all the following:

- earth (from which he was made),
- man (the male being),
- man and woman (the romantic couple), and
- mankind (the collective kind)

Therefore, man as in humankind is collectively masculinized because a woman was originally taken out of a man. The reason why God refers to Himself as "He" is also hidden in the account of man's creation. God created Adam then extracted Eve. In the grand scheme of things, the separation of male and female into distinct genders occurred unequivocally for the expression of love as well as for procreation. This is not to say women matter less than men. Such a statement would be untrue. God saw that it was not good for the man to be alone. So, He created a masterpiece whom the man could love and be loved by, become broken for, with whom he could work together, reason and unfortunately even disagree with, and bear children. Without women, the next generation could not be brought into existence. Nevertheless, male and female are still collectively male, mankind, and therefore masculine. The all-knowing God who existed before creation is also masculinized because He existed before He created that which we call female.

CHAPTER 6

Unmatched Engineer

God's creation displays a level of intricacy that is unprecedented from scale to scale. The microscopic universe is every bit as detailed as the macroscopic one. Surely, the Creator's fingerprint is everywhere, yet many fail to see the marvels of engineering that surround them. Nevertheless, the LORD God is something of a scientist! His written word agrees with provable science. The only "scientific" areas it disagrees with are the unprovable ideas that constitute the Big Bang Theory and Theory of Evolution. Not one person has ever observed a random object appear out of nowhere without a cause. However, every person has observed that all designs, structures, and machines have makers.

By far, we human beings are some of the most advanced pieces of machinery to have ever been conceived by intellect and designed by hand. Intelligent life perfuses our bodies from the smallest cells to our entire forms. Our processing capabilities when properly exercised are unrivaled even by the fastest supercomputers. Our memories can hold unfathomably large quantities of information in both knowledge and experiences. If we were to download your consciousness into a modern computer, the entirety of your being, including memories, biorhythmic schedules, processes, etcetera, you would easily overload any man-made contraption smaller than a basketball. Our internal storage and processing capabilities outclass the fastest chips and cannot be measured by current standards (gigabytes, terabytes...etc.). Moreover, unlike anything man-made, every member of our bodies has extensive abilities to self-repair. Even so, since there is a strong denial of the scientific validity of the Bible, I will explain the creation of mankind from an engineering perspective.

Man was made in six main steps:

Stage 1: The idea
Stage 2: The production of man
Stage 3: The idea of a woman
Stage 4: Sample extraction
Stage 5: Design of a woman
Stage 6: User feedback

STAGE 1: The idea

And God said, Let us make man in our image... - Gen 1:26

For this illustration, this can be categorized as part of the "concept stage", where God generated the idea of man and expressed His will or determination to develop the being.

STAGE 2: The production of man

And the LORD God formed man of the dust of the ground, and breathed into his nostrils the breath of life; and man became a living soul. - Gen 2:7

Man was the product of supernatural engineering, a fully functional prototype far more advanced than anything we will ever make or imagine! Mark those words, for it is written—we are fearfully and wonderfully made. Indeed, it is remarkable how well designed we are, right down to our cellular and molecular compositions.

STAGE 3: The idea of a woman

And the LORD God said, It is not good that the man should be alone; I will make him a helper suitable for him. - Gen 2:18

This was another concept stage in which the LORD decided He would create a helper and companion for the man.

STAGE 4: SAMPLE EXTRACTION (Borrowing an ingredient)

And the LORD God caused a deep sleep to fall upon Adam, and he slept: and he took out one of his ribs, and closed up its place with flesh; - Gen 2:21

The LORD extracted a sample from Adam showing He works efficiently. Though He could have made the woman from scratch, why would He do it that way when there was a better way?

STAGE 5: DESIGN OF WOMAN (Semi-Cloning: using the sample from the man in order to make the woman)

And from the rib, which the LORD God had taken from man, made he a woman, and brought her unto the man. - Gen 2:22

STAGE 6: USER FEEDBACK

And Adam said, This is now bone of my bones, and flesh of my flesh: she shall be called Woman, because she was taken out of Man. Therefore shall a man leave his father and his mother, and shall cleave unto his wife: and they shall be one flesh. - Gen 2:21-24

Whereas God had determined everything to be good in His sight, His creation of a woman for Adam was something that He knew Adam would benefit from and vice versa. Adam loved her from the moment he set eyes on her. The LORD knew that Adam would love Eve. Therefore, He allowed Adam to acknowledge her goodness by saying something to the following effect: "Finally, **this** creature is bone of my bones, and flesh of my flesh. Father God, your latest creation is indeed suitable for me! I will call her woman because she was directly removed from me. For this reason, men shall leave their parents to cleave to the women they marry and start new families with them. For this reason, husbands and wives shall be recognized by two hearts which beat as one."

Would you like to know what is surprisingly true about this account? EVERYTHING. We're not talking theories, but actual history backed by real science! Modern science has supported this account for several decades without even realizing it.

#1) The Deep Sleep:

The deep sleep that the LORD induced upon Adam is reminiscent of the sedation and pain blocking procedures employed during modern surgeries. How amazing is it that Moses (the claimed author of Genesis under the inspiration of God) was able to describe something conceptually too advanced for his mind to ever contemplate? He may not have understood why the deep sleep facilitated the procedure, but he believed God.

On October 16, 1846 a man named William T.G. Morton made history by demonstrating how a surgical procedure could be facilitated by first rendering a patient unconscious. God had already known this. Whereas Morton used an anesthetic, we can be certain God did not need one. The Creator has overriding authority over all creation. Nevertheless, He created every ingredient necessary for chemists to concoct anesthetics. One day we too would perform surgical operations and forget that He did it first.

#2) The extraction

While Adam was unconscious, God removed a rib. Did you know the ribs are the only bones in the human body known to fully regenerate—if removed properly during a surgical operation?

Various sources support this. One such source is Christy Lytal's article in USC News titled: "Rib regeneration studied in mammals".

#3) Cloning ... Sort of.

After removing the rib bone, God created another independently conscious human being from it. She would be Adam's companion. The first woman was derived from a man. Science supports this, pseudoscientific theories do not. Whereas the Theory of Evolution suggests that all creatures evolved from single celled life forms, proven science reveals that women only have X chromosomes, but men have X and Y chromosomes. This was part of God's wonderful design. If men did not have both X *and* Y chromosomes, then Adam would have become the first and last man to ever exist and humanity would have ceased to exist after his daughters died. The first man and every man thereafter who mates with a woman to produce offspring ensures the gender binary continues so that life can continue.

All of this does not discredit women in any way; for without them, the miracle of **new** life would not occur. Clearly, the LORD God did everything on purpose. Neither sex could procreate without the other and none is superior or inferior to the other. They were both made in God's image. This is what, Genesis 1:27 means when it says, "in the image of God created He him; male **and** female created He them." in other words, men and women are not unequal, they simply serve different functions when they must.

Truth is no less true because we ourselves have made it uncomfortable to bear. In the LORD's divine wisdom, everything that exists was extracted from Himself. Gender will not elevate a person over another in the sight of the LORD for He is not a "respecter of persons" (Acts 10:34). In other words, no one is a favorite based on looks, gender, intellect, wealth, etc.

CHAPTER 7

Origin of Love and Companionship

Many of us pretend to know what love is. We pretend so well, in fact, that we can even fool ourselves. Often, we confuse lust, selfishness, or fondness for the **idea** of being in love with actual love; but we cannot fully understand the emotion without God's example. We have heard "Love is Love" and in the right context it is, just as a bird is a bird. An eagle, however, is not a pigeon. Therefore, just as birds can be different, so can love depending on the relationship in question. For example, we can love our pets, but we are not biologically compatible with them from a reproductive standpoint. As a result, the kind of love expressed between romantic couples is not and should not be the same love expressed toward an animal.

One might argue all life is connected, we are free spirits, the other party consented, or that controlling one's "innate urges" is a form of self-betrayal and therefore dishonest. We have even heard statements such as:

THE SERPENT'S LIE

"We can't change how we were born."

Sometimes we even dare to take it one step further by blaming God:

"Well, He made me this way!"

Let it be known that God did **not** create us with sin. We **chose** to sin in the beginning. Since then, we have chosen to continue the habit of sinning. Often, we shift blame to everything else but our lack of self-control and when we do blame it, we make it seem as though nothing can be done about it.

Beloved reader, **we** make **every** one of our decisions. **We** put a face or an image to the things we like, often subconsciously, but make no mistake—all our behaviors were learned! To clarify my point, let's go back to the topic of love and lust while considering the following fact:

People who were born blind were not born with an inclination towards people of ethnic backgrounds, nor towards people of certain skin tones, or even genders. Quite frankly, if one does develop a preference, it will be based on interaction with people, and complex associations formed among sounds, touches, tastes, and smells. The development of preference requires decision-making processes how ever subtle they may be. Everyone chooses in the end. This statement may cause controversy, but let's reason together for a moment. If someone grew up in complete physical and sensory isolation from the rest of the world, that person would not know what to and what not to like, what to find attractive or repulsive. The person had not been given the opportunity to interact with the world. So, what excuse have we to say we were born with lusts so powerful they cannot be mastered? They were all learned!

Let's consider another fact. No baby has <u>ever</u> paused to check out an attractive person walking past its stroller and thought to itself, "…if only I were 18 years older…" We learn what we like, and soon the associations become reflexive and *seemingly* instinctive or subconscious, but no one is born with lust. We put a face or image to the things we like.

Lust itself is natural. It is the physical and sexual attraction necessary for finding mates for one ultimate purpose: Procreation! So, when we do not learn to subject our lusts to our spirit and when we make excuses as to why we can't subject our bodies to our control, something interesting happens. We lose control and forget we have the power to regain it! Sex addictions, fornication, adultery, and all manner of sexual deviations are born this way. In many instances, we need the help of the Lord to regain control.

Many atheists and heathens would have us believe love is anything but God-given. They are wrong. Not only is it God-given but it originates from Him and should flow through us like steady streams. Naturally, this can be challenging as we often learn to love those who agree with us and despise those who don't.

Many of us fail to realize that even with our great capacity to love, the one who is apart from God most likely will not learn how to fully and properly use this emotion. He or she will tend to be a lover of self, money, incompatible relationships, sex, drugs, etc. In general, the person will love the wrong things at the wrong times and in the wrong ways. I am no exception to this principle.

Only an entity capable of loving could have given us the gift of love. Therefore, we should look to His example and righteousness in order to better understand and practice it. Love always requires a subject or object upon which to lavish itself. For instance, Eve was the object of Adam's romantic desires.

Romantic love (at least among humans) has often been expressed between lifelong companions usually of opposite sex. For men, throughout history, it has often been a wife; for women, a husband. When the great Creator made everything, He said they were good except for one thing. It was not good for Adam to be alone.

God had made almost all creatures in pairs, male and female according to Genesis 1:27. Therefore, there were **male** birds and **female** birds to propagate their species. There were also male and female fish to do the same, as well as every other living thing on earth; and God had determined them to be good. This was before man in rebellion to the Most High began to decide for himself what he would consider "good".

God's creations had all been wonderful accomplishments in self-sustenance. Through His design, sentient and intelligent life could reproduce without our Creator populating the world creature by creature. Instead, humanity could be fruitful and multiply, to the several billions of people on Earth today. 'Male and female, He created them.' God did not feel that Adam was complete without a companion. So, He brought the animals before the man who named them. After naming each one, Adam found not one of them suitable for lifelong companionship and romance.

Adam realized that each creature already had its own specially designed mate to which it was similar and naturally attracted. But God wanted mankind to be happy. So, he put Adam to sleep and went to work creating a one-of-a-kind partner for him; one whom Adam would call "woman". Whereas our heavenly Father had created man from clay or earth, according to the Bible, He created the first woman from one of Adam's ribs.

When Adam awoke, he saw the brand-new face of the creature who had been designed specifically for him and all of humankind from that point on. He was drawn to her and instantly recognized as her to be the 'bone of his bones and flesh of his flesh'. He saw himself in her, and she saw herself in him. They were one, and yet two distinct entities.

Adam was drawn to the "feminine" part of himself which had been removed and made into a separate individual who could hug him, kiss him, have conversations with him, and start a family with him. Likewise, his companion was attracted to the part of herself which she had been removed from. Adam named her Chava (or "Eve" as English speakers know it), because she would be the "mother of all the living" (Genesis 3:20).

Whereas Eve would be more emotional and sensitive, Adam would be her strength and comfort. Whereas Adam was likely stubborn and strong, Eve would be the tenderness and reasoning he would need to bring balance and soundness to his decisions. Even so, Adam and Eve were still (in a sense) one entity merely separated into two distinct "reflections" of each other. It is here that we can discover an aspect of God that manifests itself in his creation. HE cares so deeply for us, but He also loves Himself. His creations exist for *His* glory and honor. He did NOT create us for our own sake, though he wants the best for us. He loves us as He loves Himself because we are like bits of God removed from His own self!

The Lord has proclaimed He is a jealous God. HE wants to be loved by us above all others, but as the good lover that He is, He watches mankind love him less, and fall more "in love" with money, drugs, sex, and other things. He is hurt because He is great, but our Adversary has deceived many of us into thinking otherwise. Deep down, however, our spirits know the truth. God is real and He wants us to open our eyes to see that He genuinely desires a relationship with us.

God loved Adam and wanted to bless him greatly. The LORD knew even before the animal naming event that Adam would need Eve. Even so He had a special purpose for bringing the animals before Adam. He wanted the human being to see the parity, the companionship, and the male and female design that would not only allow for the propagation of the species of the world, but would also allow living creatures to experience the fullness of romantic love in a way that could not have been experienced otherwise. He wanted Adam to know that he was the fitting piece for Eve and vice versa. He wanted love to be expressed between them, and what better way to do it than to make it an exchange between two separate entities who vibed as one? After all, how well can one hug and kiss themselves?

Most people would agree that a hug feels better from another person and this is precisely what our God wanted! I would, however, like to remind us all to remember to love our creator as well. Do not leave him out of the emotional exchange! He created love so let us keep Him in mind, loving Him appropriately as our Creator, Savior, and the one who first loved us.

CHAPTER 8

The Crafty Serpent

Shortly after the creation of Eve, a master deceiver entered the picture—a serpent who had willfully submitted himself to the evil entity Satan. The serpent had one mission in mind: to persuade Adam (not Eve) to eat from the forbidden tree. Satan, the spirit within the serpent was jealous of God's supremacy. Satan was originally created "perfect in beauty" and had held a very high-ranking position among the angels until sin was found in him. He lusted for power and had unrighteous pride.

A common misconception about the fall of Lucifer (who became Satan) is that God is ultimately to blame. Clearly this notion exists due to an inadequate understanding of how free will actually works. You see, God did create Lucifer, but Lucifer, like human beings, possessed true self-determination. He was not created with sin, but when he became prideful and sought to be like the Most High God, it manifested itself in him.

Ezekiel 28: 15 - 16 says:

15 You were perfect in your ways from the day that you were created, till iniquity was found in you.
16 By the abundance of your trading you became filled with violence within, and you sinned; therefore I cast you as a profane thing out of the mountain of God: and I destroyed you, O covering cherub, from the midst of the fiery stones.

If a created entity cannot choose its own destiny, then it **does not** have free will and it is a robot. God did not create robots. He made thinking and feeling beings. Lucifer was no different. He was therefore able to decide on a different path for himself. Out of his own power of self-determination, he became Satan (the Devil) to God and man.

Satan wishes the worst for mankind, but not because we did anything to him directly. Rather, he is in a desperate position, caught between a power hungry past to present, and a doomed future. What would you do if you were destined to suffer eternal destruction without the possibility for redemption and there was a countdown to your final hour? How would you feel knowing someone else had a hopeful future, but you didn't? You might probably try to wreak as much havoc as you could—one big middle finger to the sky. Your choices would no longer matter one way or another if your doom was inevitable.

Fortunately, God has a hopeful future for mankind. He loves every one of us and desires a relationship. In order to make that happen, we must humble ourselves and understand that He is God. Though He listens to us, and cares deeply about our quality of life, our joys, and our sorrows, His mercies will fall upon those who seek His favor.

The Devil's malevolence and opposition toward us are primarily intended to attack the heart of God! Thus, after God proclaimed His creation to be "good", Satan, working through the serpent, sought to corrupt it. Though he was originally created exceedingly beautiful, He wanted more. He wanted to be adored and worshipped! Proud and power hungry, he was cast out of Heaven and watched as human beings were made in the image of the God whose authority and power he coveted. One opportune day, as he moved through the garden of Eden, he spotted Adam and Eve.

In that era, the earth was under the rule of the human pair. The vastness of this realm was their territory. We can imagine how envious Satan became upon learning this! He began his campaign to steal Adam and Eve's dominion from them and debase the flesh-form children of the Most High. However, he would not physically harm Adam and Eve, whom God had clothed in glory; for he knew he would be easily outmatched by the LORD's vengeance, if he were to harm them. To this day, Satan knows he is no match for our all-powerful God! Yet it does not impede his evil plotting. He intends to influence man's fall by implanting ideas into his mind, such as:

- God is not all-good.
- His word is not fully trustworthy.
- He does not want what's best for us.
- He just wants us to think that He has our best interests at heart in order to control us.

These ideas are false! Satan suggested them to taint the human perception of God. He did not feel that the Most High was solely deserving of the praises of His angels and the rest of creation. Moreover, he wanted to be a god of equal or greater power, but there is only one God—the creator of the Heavens and the Earth. Furthermore, the maker of something has dominion over the made thing, not the other way around. Satan could not accept this. He was consumed by a delusion to become all-powerful.

Satan is jealous of God and his children. Sin was found in him by the very God who knows all hearts. Lucifer was blinded by his pride to think (in his heart) that he could be like the Most High. Unlike God, he was created. Unlike God, he was not self-sufficient. Unlike God, he did not possess a single item or attribute that had not been given to him.

The Bible does not say that Satan verbalized his desire to be like God, but it does suggest that he was determined to do it in his heart. Isaiah 14: 13-14 reveals Satan's sin saying:

*13 For you have said **in your heart**, I will ascend into heaven, I will exalt my throne above the stars of God: I will sit also upon the mount of the congregation, in the farthest sides of the north:*
14 I will ascend above the heights of the clouds; I will be like the most High.

As an omniscient being, God foresaw the impending rebellion before it ever took place! Satan was cast out of Heaven. Since then, he has been very busy. Through deception, he usurped the dominion that human beings once possessed as the created likeness of God. Though we had been made to rule with God on earth, Satan became the "prince of this world after he persuaded Adam and Eve to disobey God. Nowadays, he seeks to suppress the truth of the LORD God and tarnish the LORD's image, whenever he can. In this manner, he draws lost souls to himself, often without their knowledge.

Confusion has swept the world and it spreads as a product of corruption. Many, including Luciferians, demon empathizers, Satanists, and some other groups (who may or may not *explicitly* or even consciously side with the Adversary), believe Satan and his followers are misunderstood. They regard God the Creator as the villain in this story, the one who does not want people to be "happy" and live in a state of perpetual peace. They see with poor vision and could not be farther from the truth. Fornicating, indulging in drugs, becoming full of greed, coveting riches, possessions, living "carefree" lives etc. is not the route to happiness. God is not against sexual pleasures. He created them for specific purposes and with instructions for maximum enjoyment, and minimum heartbreak and guilt.

Two romantic partners should first be married and truly committed to each other before becoming sexually active with each other. That is God's ideal. That was always His desire for us. Regrettably, we tend to favor instant gratification and often end up heart broken or breaking someone's heart. We end up wondering why we always fall for the wrong people, have psychotic ex-partners, or experience marital problems. God wants us to be happy, but though He created us and knows how we operate better than we do, we like to think we know best.

Life isn't about partying like it's our last day, drinking to drown sorrows or guilt, or fornicating just because sex feels good. Every sensation was created for a good purpose and to be enjoyed at the right times, with the right people. Good sensations were never meant to be enjoyed in disobedience to God's law. When we disobey God and please our flesh, we might feel great for a moment, but guilt and or consequences soon follow. If we're wise enough, we learn to quickly realize the error of our ways. If not, we find ourselves wondering why things eventually go awry.

God is good and wants the best for us, but Satanic forces mislead and take advantage of the souls who have not yet discovered the truth. False religions have arisen as a result of the serpent's deception. For those who seek truth, rest assured you can find it in the word of the LORD. When we lean upon His word and not our own understanding, many things will begin to change in our lives. For instance, we suddenly begin to realize just how special we are to have been created in His likeness. We also begin to discover our purposes...cease to be confused and or depressed, have fellowship with Him, and live in power, love, and peace of mind.

God's likeness within us has lent itself well to our creative endeavors. We have designed enormous structures and developed amazing technologies. For instance, we have made inorganic lifeforms we call "robots", many of which are "intelligent". The very existence of these entities, even conceptually, has been a testament to the creative potential within us. Yet we often forget we make things to serve us and our purposes.

We often forget that our contraptions never ask to be brought into existence, but we make them, nonetheless. Likewise, we never asked to be brought into existence, but we were made to serve God's purposes. Isn't it concerning, then, that many people are too proud to serve their own maker?

The LORD created us with freedom to choose. Will we honor or dishonor Him? Will we serve Him or rebel? Will we love him or hate Him? Will we allow Him to love us, or will we reject Him? What will we do with that which He entrusts to us? Those decisions, dear reader, are ours to make. Either way, we exist for His glory and honor.

God respects the free will of his creatures, **but** He will not permit a revolt in His realm for the same reason we would not allow A.I. to seize control of our world (if we can help it)! Therefore, it should not be surprising that God did not tolerate mutiny in His Heavenly domain even though Satan and his rebellious angelic followers never posed a *legitimate* threat to His reign.

CHAPTER 9

Good and Evil

After sin was found in Lucifer, God immediately cast him away, knowing their former relationship was damaged beyond repair. Sometime later, when Satan saw Adam and Eve in the garden, he seized the opportunity to deceive Eve. Satan possessing a serpent said to Eve:

"...Yea, hath God actually said, 'Ye shall not eat of every tree in the garden'?" And the woman said unto the serpent, We may eat of the fruit of the trees of the garden: But the fruit of the tree which is in the midst of the garden, God hath said, Ye shall not eat of it, neither shall ye touch it, lest ye die. And the serpent said unto the woman, Ye shall not surely die: For God doth know that in the day ye eat thereof, then your eyes shall be opened, and ye shall be as gods, knowing good and evil. - Gen 3:1-5

Moments later the serpent (possessed by Satan) successfully led her to sin and caused Adam her husband to follow her, bringing death upon the world. Thus, he rendered all created things the casualties of a war between good and evil, the Kingdom of God, and the Satanic forces of Darkness and Deception.

To better understand what made Satan so effective, let us decompose and rephrase the verbal and nonverbal exchange into a more contemporary dialogue:

"Did God really say, "You shouldn't eat from every tree in the garden?" asked the serpent feigning interest. *"Hmmm...I wonder why He would say something like that?"* he said, pretending to think out loud. *"That really baffles me, Eve! ... I mean He made the trees, right?"* He continued, *"... and ... and this is your home, right?"* He looked at Eve with bewilderment. She replied, *"Well...actually, He said that we can eat from any tree we wish to eat from except from the one in the middle of the garden because its fruit is poisonous. We'll die even if we touch it!"*

After Eve explained the deadly warning concerning the knowledge fruit, Satan immediately replied to this effect: *"That's not true Eve. Is that what He told you?! How can you die from eating a fruit? Does it look any more dangerous than any other fruit you've enjoyed before?"* He manipulated her, knowing that without a strong concept of death, there was no way for her to imagine a single way to die from

THE SERPENT'S LIE

it. It was like trying to imagine a color she had never seen before! We should already know that without assistance, we cannot imagine the unimaginable until it happens.

"I mean, I suppose you could choke if you weren't careful," Satan continued, *"but what are the chances of that? Look Eve, you strike me as an intelligent woman. So, I'm sure you must've wondered why God forbids you to eat from that tree."* Eve had not wondered such a thing before. She had always just obeyed God and submitted herself lovingly to her husband Adam. She had never thought to question anything. But now, stuck and caught off guard she began to search for an answer. At last, her gaze fell upon the fruit. *"Why does God forbid it?"*, she thought. It did not seem bad nor dangerous to her. Rather, it was just as harmless as the ones she and her husband had freely eaten before. *"The serpent's right!"*, she thought. *"The fruit of this tree does not look any more dangerous than the other fruit in the garden."* Little did she know appearances can be deceiving!

Eve's pupils dilated in interest and the serpent broke his silence, saying *"God knows that when you eat from this fruit, you and your husband will be like gods! Wisdom—unimaginable to you right now—and the knowledge of good and evil are contained in each fruit."* As he spoke those words, she began to succumb to his influence. The fruit did look good for wisdom, and wisdom seemed like something one should have. Seeing she was giving in, the serpent pressed on. *"Do you think God wants you to be like Him?",* he asked. Eve could not respond. She never once realized that during her discourse with the serpent she had been allowing him to taint her perception of the character of God.

"No Eve! He doesn't want that! He wants Heaven, Earth, and all praises to Himself! Don't you see? He's selfish! He made you in His image but left you alone in this garden with rules to keep you from reaching your potential. In the meantime, He enjoys the company of His angels who sing His praises and not yours! So, go ahead sweetheart, take a bite. It's time you learned what your so-called Father is hiding from you…and how threatened He would truly feel if you became like Him."

Thus, Satan was able to deceive Eve. He neglected to mention that it would not be the fruit per se that would bring about Death. We do not die because the first human couple took a bite or two from a "knowledge fruit". However, we all die sooner or later because God spoke it. He ensured that Death would be the punishment assigned for sin, and as sorrowful as it is, it was a wise punishment. For it would not have benefited mankind to be indefinitely trapped on a cursed world with reproductive capability.

Can you imagine how much worse this world would be with its current human population, and their immortal ancestors all competing for resources and food? Could you imagine if Jesus

Christ who was born from mortal man to save the world was not able to die for anyone in an impactful way? How would we comprehend His marvelous gift of salvation and self-sacrifice if we were not acquainted with death? God loves us too much to have allowed us to live immortal lives on a depraved earth and remain in unrestorable separation from Him. Unfortunately, we are blind to this fact! He did not punish mankind with satisfaction, but He did so in utter disappointment and delivered on His promise of death. Nevertheless, He was merciful.

CHAPTER 10

Undeserved Mercy; Justified Reproach

We should know that God as a creator has every right and ability to send his wrath upon us. If this does not make sense to someone, a special dose of humility is desperately needed. We should understand that God *can* wipe out life in a horrific fashion. Moreover, we should recognize He does not desire to do so, but desires to spare us. He loves us incredibly, but He is Holy and perfectly righteous! Thus, the punishment was both just and merciful.

There are times in our lives where we willingly act against our consciences and loathe ourselves in those moments. Many of us feel like terrible human beings yet when we wake up each morning, we often take it for granted, not realizing His mercies were made new once more out of His love for us, but He does not give us infinite chances. Nobody is too young for a freak accident to end their earthly existence. Nobody is too healthy to lose their lives for any number of reasons. Fortunately for us, He enjoys being merciful.

THE SERPENT'S LIE

Adam disobeyed a simple commandment. Despite his disobedience, however, God loved him so much that He did not immediately destroy him and start afresh. Although Adam and his wife could have enjoyed access to a plethora of alternative food options, they had chosen to indulge in the only forbidden fruit.

Mankind's disobedience was the first demonstration, of the human capacity not only to choose, but to rebel against our own Creator! It reminds us that we can determine paths for ourselves which may be directly opposed to our own maker's desires for us. Despite this, the LORD spared us back then because He still has better plans for His creation (even when this world may seem hopeless at times).

Our all-powerful Father desires a wonderful relationship with us, His children. We have been given many chances to know Him and there are many ways to get acquainted. Prayer, fasting, meditation, and reading His word (the Bible) are some ways to build and strengthen a relationship with Our Lord. Meditating upon His promises both good and "bad" is also an excellent way to understand the heart of the Father which is for and not against us. Even so, the Most High punishes as a good parent does.

As a result of Adam's disobedience, our Father punished the following parties in the order of their sin: First, the Serpent, along with the Devil who had entered it, then, Eve, finally Adam.

Let's examine closely.

God cursed the serpent first because it had allowed itself to be used by Satan to deceive Eve. The serpent's lie was the stimulus that brought corruption to God's perfectly planned world.

*"And the LORD God said unto the serpent, Because you have done this, you are **cursed** above all cattle, and above every beast of the field; upon your belly shall you go, and dust shalt you eat all the days of your life."*

Before God declared the curse upon the serpent, we can infer that it had been able to travel in a manner other than slithering on its belly. In other words, it might have been able to walk and or even to fly; but surely enough, modern serpents travel on their bellies, as God said they would from that day on. Many people would call it a myth, arguing the story has no basis in fact. Strangely enough, a fascinating scientific validation of this event may exist in the fact that snakes have hip bones connected to their spine! This vestigial structure may indicate a time when serpents had limbs.

CHAPTER 11

The Old Serpent

The original serpent is part of a group of created things which I will now refer to as "the Never-seen", which include "legendary" biblical creatures like "the Leviathan", or places such as "the Heavenly Kingdom of God". These are things that have never been observed by most people.

When we try to imagine them, the Never-seen remind us that everything imaginable, is inspired by the "Seen". Every color that we know of is a color we have seen before. Even if we tried to imagine a completely original idea, we would use elements drawn from what we have observed. For instance, if you are told to imagine a monster, you might imagine its skin as scaly, furry, leathery, slimy, metallic, rocky, jeweled, etcetera. These types of material textures already exist in our world and if you were to imagine them even in an original combination, you would still draw inspiration from your mental database of past observations. My point is this… even the most far-fetched ideas are inspired by things which have been seen in this realm. Take for instance the concept of a dragon. Many cultures have stories of dragons. Where did all those stories originate? Were they seen in ancient history? Could they have been inspired by actual encounters? Perhaps.

The transformation of the serpent into a belly-crawling, dust-eating beast begs the question *"how did it look before it was cursed"*? Our answer can only be speculated at this time since the Bible does not describe its physical features. Even so, Revelation 12:9 hints at a serpent-dragon connection when it says that *"the great **dragon** was cast out, that old serpent called the Devil and Satan..."*

Have you ever wondered where stories of dragons originated? Have you ever wondered why they bear so much resemblance to the reptilian creatures that we know of? Why don't dragons look like puppies or ponies, instead of dinosaurs and other reptiles?

One need only look at pictures of Chinese dragons to see their astonishing anatomical resemblance to snakes. Is it possible that before the serpent was cursed to its belly crawling existence, it was a dragon? Absolutely!

The Bible introduces the Serpent briefly in Genesis 3:1, describing it as more cunning than any beast of the field which the LORD had made. One day, while Eve was walking through the garden, it captured her attention near the tree of the Knowledge of

Good and Evil. She was unaware that just a few moments before she encountered it, the creature had relinquished control of itself to the dark power of Satan, the true culprit behind the Fall of mankind.

The serpent specifically mentioned in Genesis, was created with all the other animals. Satan, however, existed before the serpent. Despite this fact, Revelations chapter 12 verse 9 explains that Satan **was** the serpent, although he **is not** a serpent. How can this be? The answer is simple when we understand what spirit possession truly is. Spirit possession is the ownership that a spirit has over a material body. The human being is truly a spirit inhabiting a body. We exercise temporary ownership over this body almost like the operator of a mech-suit. When we look in the mirror, we cannot see our invisible spirit, but we do see the body and face we identify with.

Whenever a spirit, especially a foreign one, enters a host to possess it, the spirit in control assumes the physical identity of the host. Thus, Satan briefly became the serpent by taking control of the its body. The Wicked One in his disguise relished the opportunity to exploit Eve's lack of knowledge. She was unaware she was speaking with the Devil. Eventually, she succumbed to the temptation and ate of the fruit. She then gave a piece to her husband who had been with her during this exchange, but one reason or another had not intervened. As soon as they both had eaten from the fruit, their eyes were indeed opened as Satan promised. Later that day, God came to the garden to check on Adam and Eve, and they hid from Him; for they had heard His voice and were afraid because of their nakedness. God knew they had sinned and now they would find out how much truer God's word was than the Devil's. God punished them according to their involvement, starting with Satan and the Serpent.

"And I will put enmity between thee and the woman" said the LORD God *"and between thy seed and her seed; it shall bruise thy head, and thou shalt bruise his heel."* - Gen 3:14-15

Prior to that moment, there had been no enmity between Eve and the serpent. Some people who are familiar with the serpent's punishment falsely believe it to be a mythological explanation for why snakes slither and why people fear them. However, the passage of scripture that explains his punishment was **not** intended to explain the origins of ophidiophobia (the fear of snakes). Not all snakes are scary.

The Genesis account is not an allegory nor a myth. It is uncorrupted history in which genealogies (the documentation of lineages and family relations) first appears in the Bible. No other belief system has managed to keep a detailed and purposeful record of family history!

God stated in Genesis 3:14-15 that enmity would result from the Fall of man but also promised to rescue humankind. The first part of this promise was to put Satan, the serpent, and the woman at odds with each other. It's not hard to imagine Eve would hold a grudge against her true beguiler as well as the animal that was used in order to beguile her. The LORD also put enmity between Satan's seed and Eve's seed. In the second part of the promise, the seed of Satan (or his followers) would be at odds with the offspring of Eve (her descendants). The third part of this promise foretold how one of Eve's descendants (the man called "Jesus") would bruise Satan's head and Satan would bruise <u>His</u> heel. Believers know this promise was referencing and foreshadowing, Christ Jesus, the Messiah, both son of God and God in flesh (and still a man because a spirit assumes the physical identity of the body it possesses).

CHAPTER 12

Eve's Sorrow and Conceptions

After the Serpent had been dealt with, God then proceeded to address Eve, for her involvement. The LORD told her:

"I will greatly multiply your sorrow and your conception; in sorrow you shall bring forth children; and your desire shall be to your husband, and he shall rule over you."

The LORD God was greatly disappointed in Eve and so subjected her to the sorrow and shame of being the first woman to fall! Can you imagine how sad and shameful it must have been? Eve had been deceived while Adam had deliberately disobeyed. The fall of mankind was Adam's fault! Nevertheless, Eve had played her part.

Eve became the first of an entire race of women to fall from glory. Consequently, as long as she would live, she was destined to feel the guilt and sorrow of bringing forth human beings into a world which was cursed in part because of her. She had lived in paradise! How could she look into her children's eyes and explain to them what they had lost and how it had been taken from them? How could she tell them how she and Adam had once been able to see and talk with their "Grand" Father (pun intended).

When the LORD God created Adam and Eve, He instructed them to be fruitful and multiply; and after they ate from the tree, He still wanted them to follow those instructions. However, Eve would now be responsible for populating the world in a mortal body. Her childbearing pains would increase in direct relation to her diminishing physical durability.

According to Genesis, Eve's frequency of childbirth increased along with the sorrow of bearing each mortal child. God had promised (while He was cursing the serpent) that her seed would crush its head). With each child, however, she became *increasingly* sorrowful, realizing that the promised redeemer had not come. God's punishment also pre-determined the dynamics of future relationships to come; Adam would be her desire and he would rule over her.

Many people believe Eve's desire for Adam was an urge to *control* him. She desired to rule over him, but he would win the power struggle. Others believe this desire was like idolatry. Eve would seek Adam's approval, his love, his attention, etc., and he would occasionally take advantage of her feelings for him. Regardless, of the interpretation, the outcome was the same. Adam would use his physical advantage and stubborn resolve to rule over her.

To this day, we see similar dynamics. How many times have we heard the saying "It's a man's world?" How often have we seen males in 'high places' whether they are in the military, law enforcement, government, and even business? Too often! This is not to say women cannot take charge and lead well. There exists a long line of women who are considered to have been great leaders in their day, for example, Cleopatra, Joan of Arc, Queen Elizabeth just to name a few. Throughout history, however, we can also find a substantially longer list of men in leadership positions and this is certainly not by accident! Thus, it is not hard to imagine how Adam became the first "head of the household".

If, we choose to interpret Eve's desire as idolizing Adam (who was most dear to her romantically), we may discover an interesting dynamic that still holds true today. Women often love men so deeply it can border on idolatry. Sadly, many men who understand this "hold" they have on the hearts of their lovers, use it to their advantage. Thus, they rule over their partners. This even explains why young women often feel the most hurt after serious heartbreak. God's original design was for men and women to have dominion (or rule) **together**. With either interpretation, we can see how God's promise of Adam's rule manifested itself in Eve's life.

After Eve's sentence had been pronounced, God proceeded to punish Adam.

CHAPTER 13

By the Sweat of the Brow

(Adam's Punishment)

Mankind's fall from glory was more Adam's fault than Eve's; for it was not until Adam (the resource from which Eve had been formed) ate of the fruit that <u>both</u> of their eyes were opened to their nakedness and to the knowledge of good and evil. It was not until Adam ate for himself that the "circuit" was completed. Adam's punishment was to toil the land. This was long before currency was established, and supermarkets were developed. It is very important for us to acknowledge how the world has changed. Life back then was not life as we know it today. These days, when most people think of "work", they think offices, computers, etc. Most people don't think of growing their own food, making their own clothes, tools, homes., etc. Instead, most of us just earn money to buy them. Nevertheless, the punishment of Adam has not changed. We live by the sweat of the brow as the LORD promised Adam.

In Genesis 3: 17-19, we read:

***17** And unto Adam he said, Because you hearkened unto the voice of your wife, and have eaten of the tree, of which I commanded you, saying, You shall not eat of it:* **cursed is the ground** *for your sake; in sorrow shall you eat of it all the days of your life;*
***18** Thorns also and thistles shall it bring forth to you; and you shall eat the herb of the field;*
***19** In the sweat of your face shalt you eat bread, till you return unto the ground; for out of it were you taken: for dust you art, and unto dust shall you return.*

Adam listened to Eve's voice and allowed her suggestion to override God's instruction. Consequently, God **cursed the ground** because of him (or "for his sake" as it is written in the King James version). Ruminate upon this for a moment.

The LORD could have wiped humankind from existence and begun anew, or cursed Adam according to the fullness of His disappointment. Instead, He stated "cursed is the ground for your sake". If this was not mercy, then I don't know what is. God knew cursing the ground would affect mankind, but He chose to curse it instead of cursing Adam (directly). Every living thing thenceforth would live and die, but death would be a blessing in disguise. For

God loved humankind so much that even in the garden, He had already promised to save us. As you may recall, He had cursed the serpent and promised vengeance upon Satan because he had deceived the couple. Then He admonished mankind and cursed the earth upon which we live. Additionally, as he expelled the pair from the garden, He prevented them from reaching for the Tree of Life because this would have worsened the situation. With that in mind, God ensured we would indeed toil but not eternally, if we accept His gift of salvation.

It can sometimes be hard to imagine how much God loves us when, every day, we hear of tragic events happening around the world to innocent people. There is suffering in this world because of its separation from the LORD, but thankfully we will not live on this cursed soil eternally separated from our maker. In cursing the serpent, the ground, and in rendering humanity (and the rest of creation) mortal, God showed mercy towards us; yet, He was more than fair and just when He punished us. You and I are the sons and daughters of a wonderful Divine Father.

After humankind's fall from glory, man was sentenced to toil and labor for sustenance. The ramifications of the first sin are still felt by all because Adam represented all humans who had yet to be born into this world. Additionally, he represented Eve who had been removed from him. Therefore, both of their eyes were opened only **after** Adam ate from the knowledge fruit. For if Eve had become ashamed of her nakedness or shown any symptoms before Adam had ever tasted of the forbidden fruit, the man might have abstained from his sin.

Prior to the great Fall, nutrition and life had abounded on the earth without the need for heavy labor. Nowadays, however, we must toil with the earth and live by the sweat of our brows.

CHAPTER 14

Omniscience

In the days when Adam and Eve dwelt in the garden, there existed another tree besides the Tree of Knowledge of good and evil: "the Tree of Life". But after the Fall of man, the LORD God prevented them from eating of its fruit. The LORD said to himself *"Behold, the man is become as one of us, to know good and evil: and now, lest he put forth his hand, and take also of the tree of life, and eat, and live forever"* - Genesis 3:22.

I believe this verse was left open-ended on purpose, an invitation for us to infer the potential ramifications.

The sentence could have easily ended with any or both of the following:

- "He and his wife will be utterly doomed and unredeemable."

- "We will then have to destroy them all."

God knew if He allowed Adam and Eve to eat of the Tree of Life, they and their descendants would be doomed. He had planned a major rescue operation but for it to work well, Death had to exist! God's mercy would be fully displayed through His plan of salvation and redemption. If humans could die and their descendants after them, then the "seed of the woman" (who was the ***man*** called "Jesus Christ") would be mortal. Jesus would die, then rise from His death to be exalted and reunited in Godship with His Father. Had man eaten from the tree of life, however, the mortal trait would not have been passed down to Jesus and He would have been unable to lay down His life —much less in a meaningful way.

Death brings heavy sorrow, but Christ's resurrection from it is an everlasting triumph. Without our familiarity with it, we would never comprehend such a sacrifice. Had Adam eaten from the tree of Life, mankind would have been eternally separated from his maker. We would have been immortals trapped in a cursed realm. For mankind's sake, God did not grant Adam an opportunity to taste from a fruit of life.

It is very important to understand that God never punishes us simply for the sake of doing so. If we look closely there is *always* a reason for any punishment He imposes. There are always lessons to be learned. For instance, we must learn to trust our Father in Heaven at His word and to trust the judgement and reasoning behind His instruction and His correction. We must keep in mind that even in punishing, our Lord is as merciful as a good all-powerful parent can be. In fact, He loves us so greatly that He planned our salvation from before the beginning of time! Time as we know it is merely a construct that facilitates our experience of our present reality. God, however, dwells both within this construct and outside of it. Therefore, even from everlasting, He did not want humankind to be utterly doomed and unredeemable. He also did not want to have to destroy His created likeness on earth. Nevertheless, as a God of Integrity, He had to punish according to His warning. With death unleashed upon creation, our bodies are transient, but the redeemed soul will live forever with the LORD.

In the beginning, God created the Heavens and the Earth. While the Heavens had been completed before the earth and structured with rules and hierarchies, the earth of the Genesis account was amorphous and empty, a formless and desolate tohubohu, or state of chaos. The Spirit of the LORD hovered pensively over the waters of the deep before He called forth light to dispel the darkness. He had an ambitious idea in mind, one which would take six days, even for Him, to complete.

One of God's first acts was to part waters from waters in order that the dry land of this realm might appear. Detail by detail, he added to the world, plants, wildlife, stars, but He wanted more than just a stunning visual product. The LORD wanted the earth to be well maintained.

The Heavens had already been a well-designed kingdom—fruitful and rich in glory; and it had been a great home to Him as well as His angels. Although an internal conflict had arisen between God and His own precious cherub Lucifer sometime before the completion of the world, the mutiny was swiftly dealt with when Satan was cast out of the Heaven. Aside from this, however, the kingdom of God had never ceased to be rich in splendor and replete with joy. The LORD wanted the earth to be similarly managed and filled with joyful life. The newly formed realm would need an image like His to care for it and to rule over it and the LORD would develop these beings with love and care.

God's intent is to grow His kingdom and expand it for His glory and honor. Building anything requires love and commitment. So, when the LORD made mankind in His likeness and with free will, He created entities whom He could love and be loved by, and He created beings who would love and be loved by one another.

While Satan detests the image of God and His created likeness and will gladly lead us to our self-destruction, God will lead us to fulfillment! Flawed as we are, He loves us and desires to draw us back to Him, but we are often kept away by the things our Adversary has to offer; after all, it's hard to resist promises of riches, seductive partners, exotic houses, power, fame, etc. Clearly, we have not learned since eating from the Knowledge fruit—the worst things for us are often the most tantalizingly packaged, so-wrong-they-feel-right things. It is not terrible to want wealth, health, success, beautiful people in our lives and blessings. It is, however, unfortunate when many pursue, success and wealth at the expense of their souls, or have extramarital affairs at the expense of their marriages and the integrity of their families.

When we feed addictions, they distract us from the truth: our Heavenly father is a whole lot closer than we think He is. He sees what we do and although He has forgiven us for our faults, He made a way for us to leave our sinful ways behind. This does not imply we will never sin again—we are human, but His salvation comes with the assumption that we will commit to constant improvement.

The LORD our God does not want us to continue along the paths that lead to destruction—drinking, doing drugs, fornicating, lying, stealing, cheating, lusting, etc. The ground bore witness to the fall and was cursed for Adam's sake so that Adam (man and woman or humankind) would not be cursed — at least to the extent that he could have been. As a result, of the malediction upon the ground, we have had to "defile" it, not only to acquire the resources we've needed to develop modern civilizations, but also to force enough sustenance from it in order to satisfy billions of the earth's inhabitants. We toil it and it produces incomplete and corrupt nourishment. The existence of corruption and decadence are reasons why we should bless things, like our food, the lives of our families and friends, etc.; for everything in existence is connected to what we can call ***spirit engines***, the invisible and intangible drivers of the physical realm.

The manifestation of a curse, for instance, is a result of interaction with spirit engines which drive the visible reality we know. When we bless things like our food or even bless one another, the blessings interact with the spirit engines of those objects. When we do so in Jesus' name and with the right intent, the blessing is amplified.

To many, the "Fall of Man" may seem like fantasy or a fairy tale, but once upon a time, we did not believe in randomness. Our moral compasses were not "out-of-whack". We did not question so frequently the necessity for boundaries between what God considers good and that which He considers evil. Now, however, we are lost and often don't understand what has truly happened. Many who come across the scripture read it in bitterness and denial.

God has always loved us, but nevertheless, He has always been unwaveringly righteous. We all were born into a sinful world and we all have sinned. Not one person has proven themselves worthy to be glorified. God knew after the Fall of mankind; it would be impossible for any human being to live blamelessly and without sin.

In modern times, there has been a rapid increase in world problems despite the rapid increase in our knowledge. Those who realize that the answer to our problems is not human beings in places of power nor artificial intelligence, have a head-start when it comes to seeking God and living a life of blessing and purpose. Instead of turning to other human beings who are corruptible, lustfully indulgent, and fallible, we should be seeking fellowship with our LORD. There are a few hindrances however, the biggest of which is pride. God desires humility from us for we are not perfect, but He is.

CHAPTER 15

The Perfect Design… Sort of …

"Why would a perfect God have created imperfect beings?"

Satan wants us to think God is not all-knowing nor perfect. As our enemy, he accomplishes his objective by manipulating us into poorly using our individual and collective "intelligence" when it comes to God-related topics. This is true for both believers and non-believers.

When it comes to dealing with Satan, we should first understand he is still our intellectual superior. We are dealing with an entity who has existed far longer than we have; an entity who can outwit any human being with ease, sometimes turning our intelligence against us.

It is okay to question. In fact, healthy curiosity is a good thing. We must, however, be humble in asking. A question posed with the intention of invalidating God's word, is meaningless to ask. So, when we desire to know an answer, let us ask legitimately, and with humility; for it is an act of mockery to ask questions on any topic with no true intention of learning.

Any question asked in faithful expectation will be answered in due time. Bearing this in mind, I once asked the Lord, if He made the world perfect, then why are things so awry? Many have been told that God created all things perfect. Yet for such a perfect design, the reality we know seems far from perfect from our perspective. Therefore, a better question might be "What event, or factors could have ruined a perfect design?" This one assumes the validity of what many believers have been told about the Bible in a true-until-proven-false approach. From there, we can use our intelligence productively and create some simple scenarios.

For instance, suppose you create a perfect creature that can make decisions and even decide its fate. You then give it a set of instructions and it chooses to violate them. Would the violation indicate it was poorly made? ... It certainly would not. After all, it was given the ability to make its own choices; so, it did precisely that! Now suppose you had explained the consequences beforehand. Would you then be responsible for the creature's decision one way or another? Not one bit!

The LORD had commanded Adam (and Eve) not to eat of the forbidden fruit, otherwise their immortality would end in that day. However, the serpent's goal, was to taint the image of God and to make man challenge our Heavenly Father's authority. So, he capitalized on every word of Eve's reply, including her error in adding that they should not even touch the fruit (lest they die).

And the woman said unto the serpent, We may eat of the fruit of the trees of the garden: But the fruit of the tree which is in the midst of the garden, God hath said, Ye shall not eat of it, neither shall ye touch it, lest ye die.

God did not say "neither shall ye touch it". This was added by Eve.

Now, if you've been paying close attention, the fact that I said "Eve's error" may have left you wondering how a supposedly perfect creature could have made a mistake before she had ever fallen from glory? After all, perfect beings do not make mistakes, do they? I am sure some have just begun to rejoice that I have proven "the fallacy of the Bible" or highlighted another contradiction! Others, are probably wondering whose side I am on and are asking themselves what happened to the "true-until-proven-false approach" I had mentioned earlier? I posed the following question:

"What event could have ruined a perfect design?"

And now,

"What if the design had never actually been perfect in the first place?"

What a shift in thinking!

While some might see Eve's error as another place where God's word has contradicted itself, there is no contradiction in God's untarnished word. All supposed contradictions that exist have been the result of intentional and unintentional additions to and subtractions from the Holy scriptures, as well as our conditioned ways of thinking. Therefore, if you ask me whose side I am on, it's the side of truth. When God created the Heavens, the Earth, and everything in them, **the Bible said** He saw that they were—not "perfect" (as *we* have added), but— **"good"** and **"very good"**. This is not to say He was and is incapable of creating everything perfectly, but the LORD our God had a plan and brace yourself because the following revelation is POWERFUL!

THE SERPENT'S LIE

Deficiency was inherent and even crucial to His design, largely because learning beings, like humans, often discover things through trial and **error**. We cannot learn if we already know and we cannot develop if there is no room for improvement. Therefore, only an omniscient being, perfect in intelligence can get all things right the first time around. For this reason, when God made us, He did not lie about the quality of His work. He knew we were not perfect, and so He saw us as "good".

Mankind was not intended to be omniscient, nor flawless like the Supreme One. We were simply created with the potential to improve. We learn by improving upon that which we know.

I have been around enough Christian brothers and sisters to know I struck a nerve with some believers out there. This idea challenges the structural integrity of what many have firmly believed. As mentioned earlier in this book, with age, we become more rigid in our thinking; our programming becomes harder to change. As a result, when people encounter ideas that contradict what they were taught and have believed strongly in for so long, they do not know how to respond, sometimes resulting in anger, insult, scoffing, and mockery.

I am not seeking to reduce God's power in the eyes of His children, for He cannot and will not be reduced by the disclosure that a perfect God can make imperfect things. Here's an interesting factoid:

Even expert singers can intentionally hit notes we perceive to be off-key. With that said, let us revisit the opening question of this chapter:

"How could a perfect God have created imperfect beings?"

Better yet,

"Why would a perfect God have chosen to create imperfect beings?"

There was never an expectation that we would know everything which is right and wrong. We were intentionally created to learn and improve. We were made to obtain knowledge, wisdom, virtues, and other good qualities. An ideal way to learn those things, would have been through obedience to God's word. Without disobedience, sin would not have entered this world and God's perfection would have perpetually redeemed mankind without the need for a single sacrifice.

THE SERPENT'S LIE

In high school, I studied Latin and when I learned the etymology of the word "perfect", it immediately became one of my favorite words. You see, "perfect" means thoroughly done or completed, from "per" (which means "thoroughly") and the past tense of the Latin verb "facere" (meaning "to make or do"). While creation had been made good, the hierarchies and interplays were "perfect" under the LORD God Almighty. The design of the world was "good". Likewise, the design of man in the likeness of God was also "good" when God made Him. Even so, however, the things which were created in Genesis were not said to be "perfect" because they would never be perfect on their own. They would only be perfect so long as every aspect of their being remained in accordance with the will and desires of the LORD.

The learning species called human beings could approximate Godliness by following in the ways of their perfect Heavenly Father. While man was unaware of the knowledge of good and evil, he could do no wrong in God's eyes when he was without sinful thought. The serpent, knowing mankind was not perfect, knew he could easily manipulate and deceived Eve. "Your eyes will be opened, and you will be as gods" ...

He was cunning, and the first couple's curiosity was their undoing. As Adam's teeth sank into the fruit, notions began flooding both of their minds. Strange changes began to occur, and both of their eyes were indeed opened. The serpent was right! They had lived in blissful ignorance, a lower level of awareness out of which the fruit now propelled them. The short-lived trip of cognitive development ended abruptly. They looked at each other and suddenly realized something sinister had occurred. The glory which had surrounded them up until that point, had departed from them. They now stood before each other, self-consciously naked, mortal, and afraid.

A Message to the Reader:

If you enjoyed this book, please share it with your friends and family. Writing it was an incredible mental and spiritual journey for me and I sincerely hope it strengthened your faith in our true and living God. I believe firmly that we serve one who rewards those who diligently seek Him (as Hebrews 11:6 says).

Thank you for embarking on this journey with me. I look forward to many more journeys with you. In the meantime, I do blog as well, so feel free to visit the following website:

www.mysoulhaven.com

With respect to my next book, rest assured, dear reader, I am working tirelessly on the next project as Christ gives me strength.

May the LORD bless you abundantly.

-Miguel A. Valembrun Jr.

The Immortal Cell Conjecture

Blog by Miguel A. Valembrun Jr.

What if you had only one mortal cell in your body and the remaining 99% of your cells were immortal? Would natural death be a possibility in your future? Not a chance! You would only have to wait for that one cell and all its descendants to die and the immortal cells would continue to sustain your existence forever.

Now let's suppose that only 50% of your cells were immortal, would you be mortal? Not likely. After all, mortal cells can only self-divide a limited number of times with little to no defects or copy errors before they eventually die. Then your dead cells would leave your existence up to the immortal cells.

Finally, let's introduce a more extreme scenario. What if only one of your cells were immortal and the rest were mortal. Would you be mortal or immortal? This is the mystery from which the Immortal Cell Conjecture was conceived. The conjecture assumes that even one immortal cell inhabiting a living creature would give it a chance at immortality. Unfortunately, actual experimentation is currently impossible because no mortal being has access to immortal cells. Nevertheless, we *do* have access to the power of critical thinking!

One immortal cell could theoretically make us immortal if it were given enough time to reproduce and replace dead cells before the body also died.

Why all of this matters:

Once we better understand the possible implications of one immortal cell inhabiting the body of a human being, we can better understand what happened to Adam in the garden of Eden. By Adam, I do mean the earth, Adam (the man), Adam and Eve (the romantic couple), and Adam (all of humankind); for the name Adam means all of those. Furthermore, the earth, the man, the couple, and all of humanity are affected by mortality.

Had God permitted even one cell to remain immortal, death may not have been as certain as the LORD promised in the book of Genesis. God knew exactly what He was doing in the garden of Eden. Death is consistent and does not show favoritism. All life will be subject to it until Christ returns! Those who have accepted Christ as their Lord and Savior, however, share in the hope of eternity with our God.

Dear reader, if you liked what you read thus far, please feel free to visit www.mysoulhaven.com *for more...*

MAV JR.

Copyright © 2018 Miguel A. Valembrun Jr.

All rights reserved.

ISBN: 978-1-950773-00-8

www.ingramcontent.com/pod-product-compliance
Lightning Source LLC
Chambersburg PA
CBHW032303150426
43195CB00008BA/555